Letterland

My name is

....

Let's learn about...

ge gi gy   kn ch e

-tion -ture   all al-

full -ful   -le -ing -ed

Level 3 - Workbook 2

Draw lines from Gentle Ginger to the things that include her saying **ge**. Circle the one that doesn't.

Think of an **ge** word and draw it.

Write **ge** on the lines to complete these words then match them to the correct pictures.

pa _____ •   •

oran _____ •   •

ca _____ •   •

villa _____ •   •

_____ m •   •

Draw lines from Gentle Ginger to the three words with **gi** in them. Circle the one that doesn't.

Write **gi** or **ge** on the lines then read the sentence to a friend. Colour the picture.

This ___raffe likes to

eat lots of ve___tables.

Write **gi** on the lines to complete these words then match them to the correct pictures.

_____ ant •

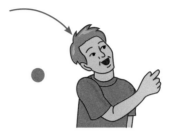

_____ nger •

•

•

_____ raffe •

•

ma _____ c •

Draw lines from Gentle Ginger to the three words with **gy** in them. Circle the one that doesn't.

Think of an **gy** word and draw it.

Write **gy** on the lines to complete these words then match them to the correct pictures.

___ m ___ •

aller ___ •

E ___ pt •

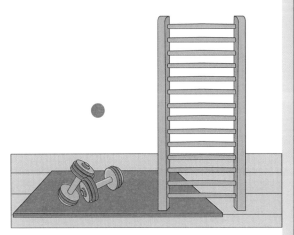

___ mnast ___ •

Sort the following soft **g** words into the correct boxes.

engineer orange manager

gymnast ginger tangerine

surgeon vegetable ginseng

Jobs	Food

Draw a line around the **ge**, **gi** and **gy** words in the grid below. They go across and down.

g	e	l	g	g	c	e	g
g	g	z	b	i	p	l	i
y	k	l	i	r	d	e	a
m	d	r	c	a	n	m	n
n	n	k	d	f	w	z	t
a	h	a	c	f	v	t	e
s	s	j	l	e	h	k	x
t	e	n	e	r	g	y	r

gymnast

giant

giraffe

gel

Can you find one more **gy** word in the grid? Copy it on to the lines.

_____ _____ _____ _____ _____ _____

Some words end in **dge.** You won't hear Dippy Duck as she's too dazzled by Gentle Ginger's gymnastics to speak! Write **dge** on the lines to complete these words. Then match them to the correct pictures.

bri _____   •

he _____   •

fri _____   •

ba _____   •

Look at the pictures and write in the **dge, ge**, **gi** and **gy** words to complete the crossword!

6   8

5

1

7   2

3

4

Across ⟶

Down ↓

Vegetables!

The Letterlanders are in the garden growing vegetables.
Join the clues and the correct vegetable with a line.
Look up any words you don't know in a dictionary.

celery   they are small, green, and grow in a pod

peas   it's long, green and crunchy

carrot   it's yellow and grows on a cob

cabbage   it's long and orange

sweetcorn   it's red or green and can be spicy!

chilli pepper   it's green and leafy

Use your stickers to label the picture below. Look back in your book if you need help remembering the words.

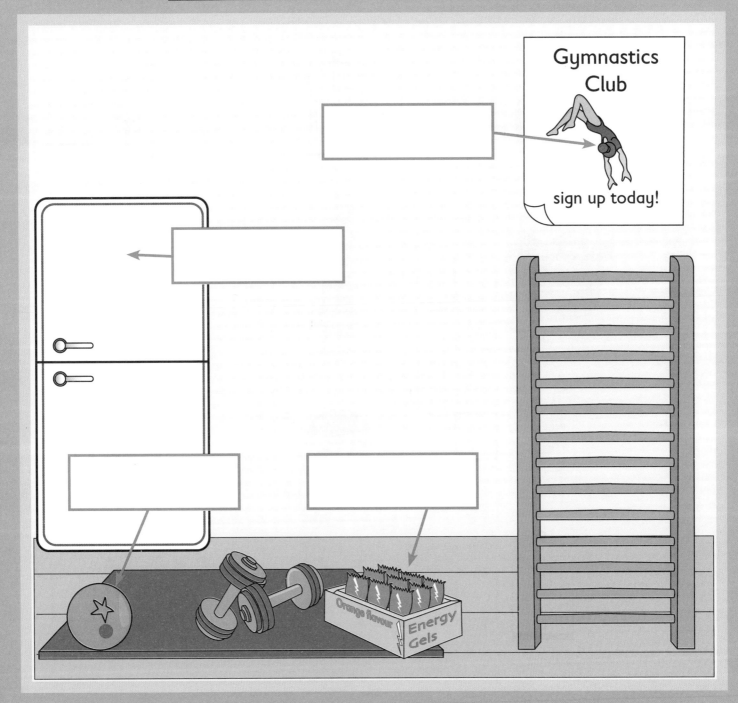

Write down where this scene is.

At the _____ .

Listen

Listen to the words and put a tick next to the one you hear. The first one has been done for you.

 Track 78

1.   ✓   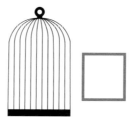 ☐    ☐

2.  ☐    ☐   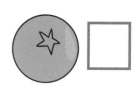 ☐

3.  ☐    ☐    ☐

4. 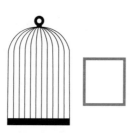 ☐   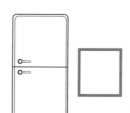 ☐    ☐

5. 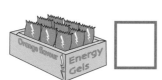 ☐    ☐   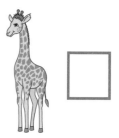 ☐

Listen again

This exercise requires careful listening skills. Listen more than once if you need to.

Listen to the words. Put a tick next to the correct spelling pattern. The first one has been done for you.

How do you spell it?

1.  ☐  ☐  ✔ 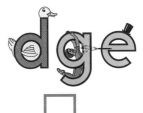 ☐

2.  ☐  ☐  ☐ ☐

3.  ☐  ☐  ☐ ☐

4.  ☐  ☐  ☐ ☐

5.  ☐  ☐  ☐ ☐

Listen again

This exercise requires careful listening skills. Listen more than once if you need to.

Draw lines from Kicking Kicking and Noisy Nick to the things that have Kicking King staying silent and Noisy Nick making noise! Circle the one that doesn't.

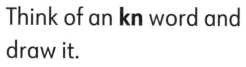

Think of an **kn** word and draw it.

Draw a line around the **kn** words in the grid below. They go across and down.

k	n	i	g	h	t	k
f	k	j	o	e	h	n
b	n	k	n	o	w	i
m	i	v	g	r	e	f
r	t	m	f	a	i	e
h	k	n	o	t	b	s

knit

knot

knight

knife

Can you find one more **kn** word in the grid? Copy it on to the lines.

____ ____ ____ ____

Fill in the missing words to complete the sentences.
The words you need are in the yellow space below.

At _____ , the

_____ likes to fight.

She _____

how to _____ .

knows   night   knight   knit

Look at the pictures and read the sentences below. Copy the correct sentence for each picture onto the lines.

- **The knight is kneeling.**
- **The knitting is in knots.**
- **He knows he has to knock.**

_____

_____

_____

_____

_____

_____

Draw lines from Clever Cat and Harry Hat Man to the things that have Clever Cat talking and Harry too startled to speak. Circle the one that doesn't.

Think of an **ch** word and draw it.

Look at the pictures below. Tick a box for each difference in picture 2 and circle them on the picture.

Write **ch** on the lines to complete these words. Add a
wind symbol to show when Harry's hat has blown off.
Leave it blank if you can hear Clever Cat sneezing.
The first line has been done for you.

 pea_c_h_

 _c_hoir

 ___eese

 ___air

 a___e

 ___ick

 s___ool

 or___id

Look at the pictures and write in the **ch** words to complete the crossword!

4

5

6

1

2

3

Across →

Down ↓

Draw lines from Mr Mean-E to the things that include him being mean. Circle the one that doesn't.

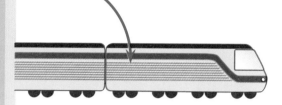

Think of a Mean Mr-E word and draw it.

Draw a line around the **e** /a/ words in the grid below. They go across and down.

s	e	a	a	b	s	e	i	l	m
a	i	z	p	b	s	l	i	o	j
c	g	l	o	n	l	s	s	p	j
t	h	r	f	r	e	i	g	h	t
i	t	k	s	s	i	p	l	a	d
o	s	p	e	w	g	a	e	d	s
g	r	e	y	s	h	c	x	w	c
y	u	i	n	e	s	p	r	e	y

Colour a star for each word you find.

☆ eight   ☆ sleigh   ☆ freight

☆ grey   ☆ prey   ☆ abseil

Write **e** or **a** on the lines to complete these words.

Note: These words are homophones. They sound the same but are spelled differently and mean different things.

e   a

___ight

e   a

___te

e   a

pr__y

e   a

pr__y

Look at the pictures and read the sentences.
Copy the correct word for each picture onto the lines.
Then colour the pictures.

eighteen   eight   eighty

He is holding _____ eggs.

It's her birthday! She is _____.

I have a letter to post at number _____.

Time for School

The Letterlanders are at school. Do you know what time things happen in your school day? Read and answer the questions.

New vocabulary!

Look at the different ways of saying the time.

five o'clock
five a.m. (morning)
five p.m. (afternoon)

quarter past five
or
five fifteen

half past five
or five-thirty

quarter to six
or five forty-five

Draw the correct time on the clocks!

Mr Mean-E gets up at eight o'clock. He does not go to school.

Vicky Violet goes to orchestra at five past nine.

Tess teaches chemistry at half past ten.

Clever Cat goes to choir at three p.m.

Quarrelsome Queen holds a quiz at quarter past three.

Firefighter Fred teaches football at four-thirty.

Use your stickers to label the picture below. Look back in your book if you need help remembering the words.

Write down where this scene is.

At the _____.

Read each sentence. Look at the other words and see if you can substitute words to make two new sentences.

| The girl is in the school. | mechanic | knight | choir | sleigh |

Example: The mechanic is in the sleigh.

....

....

....

| It is his first birthday. | eighth | eighteenth | school | ache |

....

....

....

| The cat has a mouse. | osprey | prey | knight | its |

....

....

....

| I can hear a knock at the door. | see | choir | knight | grey |

....

....

....

Read aloud Check that the new sentences you have made make sense by reading them aloud to a partner.

Listen Listen to the words and put a tick next to the one you hear. The first one has been done for you.

Track
93

1. **8** ☑ ☐ ☐

2. ☐ ☐ ☐

3. ☐ ☐ ☐

4. ☐ ☐ ☐

5. ☐ ☐ ☐

Listen again

This exercise requires careful listening skills. Listen more than once if you need to.

Listen to the words in context. Put a tick next to the correct spelling pattern. Think carefully!

 Track 94

How do you spell it?

1.  ☐   ☐

2. ☐   ☐

3. ☐   ☐

4.  ☐   ☐

5. ☐   ☐

6. ☐   ☐

7. ☐   ☐

8. ☐   ☐

Listen again   This exercise requires careful listening skills. Listen more than once if you need to.

33

Draw lines from Mr 'Tion to the things that include him saying **tion**. Circle the one that doesn't.

Draw something that has Mr 'Tion in it!

Write **tion** on the lines to complete these words then match them to the correct pictures.

por_____ •

informa_____ •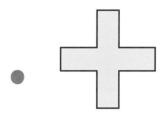

addi_____ •

celebra_____ •

pollu_____ •

Read the sentences. Then put a tick in the matching box.

He was lost, so he asked for directions.

 ☐

 ☐

He is eating a big portion of cake.

 ☐

 ☐

The city has lots of pollution.

 ☐

 ☐

Draw a line around the four **tion** words in the grid below. They go across and down.

f	r	a	c	t	i	o	n
g	r	d	q	b	p	l	p
a	x	d	d	n	d	s	o
c	d	i	d	c	n	s	r
t	i	t	e	s	w	p	t
i	s	i	s	w	e	a	i
o	g	o	w	s	h	c	o
n	v	n	i	t	b	o	n

fraction

portion

addition

action

Can you think of and write one more **tion** word on the line below.

Draw lines from Talking Tess sneezing **ture** to the things that include her that **ture** sound. Circle the one that doesn't.

Think of an **ture** word and draw it.

Look at the pictures below. Tick a box for each difference in picture 2 and circle them on the picture.

1

2

Write **ture** on the lines to complete these words then match them to the correct pictures.

furni_____ •   •

vul_____ •   •

pic_____ •   •

punc_____ •   •

pas_____ •   •

Look at the pictures and read the sentences.
Copy the correct word for each picture onto the lines.
Then colour the pictures.

furniture   picture   sculpture

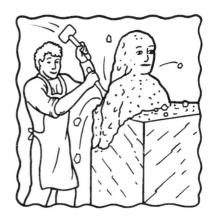

This man is making

a _____ .

They are looking at

the _____ .

The van is full of

_____ .

Draw lines from Giant All to the things that include him saying his name **all**. Circle the one that doesn't.

Think of an **all** word and draw it.

Look at the pictures and write in the **all** words to complete the crossword!

5

6

1

2   4

3

Across ⟶

Down ↓

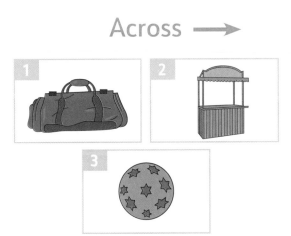

Write two **all** words to decribe each picture below.

wall   tall   hall   ball   small   call

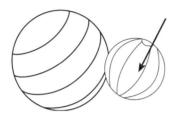

_____   _____

_____   _____

Write **al** on the lines to complete these words.

___so   ___ready

___most   ___though

___ways   ___together

Fill in the missing words to complete the sentences. The words you need are in the yellow space below.

I _____ brush my teeth

and _____ brush my hair in

the morning.

I have _____ finished this

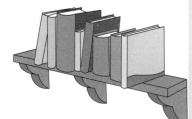

book, and I have _____

finished all those books!

also   always   already   almost

Draw lines from Giant Full to the things that include him resting on words. Circle the one that doesn't.

Think of a **-ful** word and draw it.

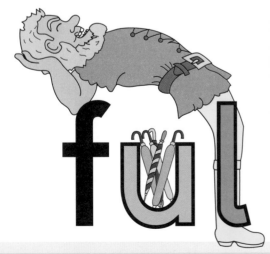

Draw a line around the -**ful** words in the grid below. They go across and down.

p	l	a	y	f	u	l	s
h	a	n	d	f	u	l	p
g	r	l	d	n	d	s	o
v	m	r	d	c	n	s	o
i	f	k	e	s	w	p	n
o	u	p	s	w	e	a	f
n	l	j	w	s	h	c	u
m	o	u	t	h	f	u	l

armful

handful

mouthful

spoonful

Can you find one more -**ful** word in the grid?
Copy it on to the lines.

___ ___ ___ ___ ___ ___ ___

Read the sentences. Then put a tick in the matching box.

She is careful when she is painting.

His stomach looks painful.

He has a nice, big mouthful of apple.

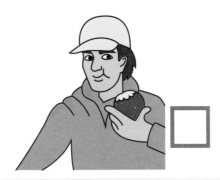   

Look at the pictures. Choose the correct **-ful** word to complete the sentences and write it on the line.

A pick-up truck is

_____ .

mouthful

useful

painful

The flowers are

_____ .

painful

beautiful

helpful

This kitten is always

_____ .

playful

careful

spoonful

The Letterlanders are in a gallery full of wonderful creations. Search the picture for the things listed on the right. Then expand your vocabulary. Use a dictionary to discover the names of things you don't know.

New vocabulary!

donation

To give something of value to help a person or organisation.

exhibition

A display of art or items of interest.

preservation

To look after something and keep it in its original state

Can you see:

a sculpture? ☐

the Queen asking questions? ☐

a collection of modern pictures? ☐

a roomful of Roman things? ☐

a monster with a mouthful of sign? ☐

an exhibition of elephants? ☐

Use your stickers to label the picture below. Look back in your book if you need help remembering the words.

Write down one more -ful word you can see in this scene.

Read each sentence. Look at the other words and see if you can substitute words to make two new sentences.

| He has a mouthful of crisps. | jam | handful | spoonful | She |

Example: He has a handful of crisps.

| There's a ball on the wall. | information | vulture | furniture | picture |

| I have already finished the book. | almost | also | spoonful | picture |

| This is a sculpture of vultures. | picture | handful | seeds | portion |

Read aloud

Check that the new sentences you have made make sense by reading them aloud to a partner.

53

Listen  Listen to the words and put a tick next to the one you hear. The first one has been done for you.

Track 114

Listen again This exercise requires careful listening skills. Listen more than once if you need to.

How do you spell it?

1.  tion ☐   sh ☐   ch ☐

2. sh ☐   ch ☐    ture ☐

3. all ☐    or ☐   aw ☐

4. aw ☐   al ☐   au ☐

5. al ☐   all ☐    ful ☐

Draw lines to all the things with Candle Magic **le**.
Circle the one that doesn't.

Think of an **le** word
and draw it.

Look at the pictures below. Tick a box for each difference in picture 2 and circle them on the picture.

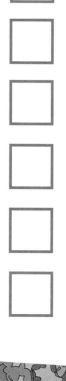

1

2

Answers: 1. The eagle has moved; 2. The jelly has changed colour; 3. The apple has disappeared; 4. The stable door has closed; 5. There is another picnic table; 6. The noodle bowl has changed colour.

Circle the **le** word that rhymes in each row.

candle

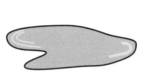

puddle

handle

apple

table

stable

apple

wobble

noodle

goose

wobble

doodle

puddle

eagle

candle

huddle

Fill in the missing words to complete the sentences. The words you need are in the yellow space below.

The horse in the

_____ would like

to eat an _____ .

Look! Ben is _____ to

play the _____ .

apple   able   bugle   stable

Draw lines from the Magic **ing** ending to the things that include it. Circle the one that doesn't.

Think of an **ing** word and draw it.

What are these Vowel Men doing? Match the sentences to the correct pictures. Use a dictionary to look up the meanings of words you don't know.

- Mr I is sliding.

- Mr A is skating.

- Mr O is dozing.

- Mr E is competing.

Best Friends to the Rescue. The magic has been stopped in all these -**ing** words. Read each row, then underline the word that does not rhyme.

 dripping   **skipping**   **sitting**    **tripping**

 **clapping**   **flapping**   **hopping**    **napping**

 **hopping**    **chopping**    **running**   **mopping**

 knitting   **sitting**   **hitting**   **biting**

Look at the pictures and read the sentences below. Copy the correct sentence for each picture onto the lines.

- She is humming and running.
- They are sitting and chatting.
- She is sitting and knitting.

Say the words and listen carefully to the ending.
Circle the word ending in **ed** that does not sound
the same.

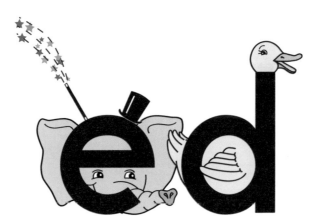

Think of an **ed** word
and draw it.

Look at the pictures and write in the **ed** words to complete the crossword!

1

5

2 →

4 ↓

6

3

Across →

1

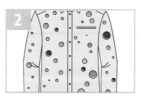
2

3

Down ↓

4

5

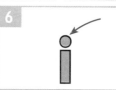
6

Say the words and listen carefully to the ending.
Circle the word ending in **ed** that does not sound
the same.

Think of an **ed** word
and draw it.

Match the first part of the sentence to the second part.
How many sentences can you make that make sense?
Read them to your partner.

Write the alphabet   smiled at me.

I was surprised that he   saved the cat.

I know you   on lined paper.

The kind girl   phoned home.

Say the words and listen carefully to the ending.
Circle the word ending in **ed** that does not sound
the same.

Think of an **ed** word
and draw it.

Read each sentence. Look at the other words and see if you can substitute words to make two new sentences.

She baked the cake.	stroked	her	scraped	knee

Example: She stroked her knee.

....

....

....

The crocodile snapped!	man	stick	baked	A

....

....

Match the first part of the sentence to the second part.
How many sentences can you make that make sense?
Read them to your partner.

I was shocked when   she was quite relaxed.

I scraped my knee   on a rock.

After stroking the cat   the crocodile snapped.

Read aloud Check that the new sentences you have made make sense by reading them aloud to a partner.

69

Look at the **ed** words. Say the word, then match it to the sound you hear at the end of the word. The first one has been done for you.

locked

lined

stroked

phoned

voted

smiled

spotted

Draw a line around the words ending in **ed** in the grid below. They go across and down.

s	e	a	a	b	s	f	a	d	e	d
p	i	z	p	b	m	l	i	o	v	s
o	g	l	o	n	i	s	s	p	w	a
t	h	r	f	r	l	i	g	h	s	v
t	t	b	a	k	e	d	l	a	a	e
e	s	p	e	w	d	a	e	d	n	d
d	s	t	r	i	p	e	d	w	h	c
y	u	i	n	e	s	p	r	e	f	y

Colour a star for each word you find.

⭐ spotted   ⭐ striped   ⭐ faded

⭐ smiled   ⭐ baked   ⭐ saved

Counting on the farm

The Letterlanders are farming! Search the picture for the things listed on the right. Then try to expand your vocabulary. Use a dictionary to find the names of any actions you don't know.

Count how many of the things listed you can find. Discuss, and write your answers on the lines.

birds ....

puddles ....

Discuss your answers with a friend.

Letterlanders holding something

Can you see:

Sammy Snake smiling? ☐

a horse in a stable? ☐

Red Robot running? ☐

Peter Puppy pulling on a handle? ☐

Dippy Duck swimming? ☐

Talking Tess driving a tractor? ☐

Use your stickers to label the picture below. Look back in your book if you need help remembering the words.

Write down the name of the bird you see.

It is an _____ .

Read Read the story once on your own. Then read it again out loud to your partner. Then listen and follow as your partner reads it to you.

Yesterday, I got out of bed, I brushed my hair, I washed my face.

Then I raced to the park.

As I was running I spotted a horse in a stable. I stopped and picked up an apple to give to the horse. I stroked the horse and smiled.

Write Write down three things you did yesterday.

Listen

Listen to the words. Put a tick next to the correct spelling pattern.

Track
135

How do you spell it?

1. ☐    ☐   ☐

2. ☐   ☐   ☐

3. ☐   ☐    ☐

4. ☐   ☐   ☐

5. ☐   ☐   ☐

Listen again

This exercise requires careful listening skills.
Listen more than once if you need to.

Listen

Listen to the words and put a tick next to the one you hear. The first one has been done for you.

Track 136

1. ✔ ☐  ☐

2.  ☐ ☐ ☐

3.  ☐ ☐  ☐

4.  ☐  ☐  ☐

5.  ☐ ☐  ☐

Listen again

This exercise requires careful listening skills. Listen more than once if you need to.

Reading and writing test

Read the questions and draw lines to match them to the answers. The first one has been done for you.

How can I cross the river?   Just lift the handle.

How do I open the window?   Go over the bridge.

What is the rocket for?   I have a pocketful!

Do you like art?   To get into space.

How many acorns do you have?   Yes! I love pictures and sculptures.

Complete these sentences using the words at the bottom.

1. Please light the _____ at the dinner _____.

2. Using _____ paper helps me keep my writing neat.

3. The train is loaded with _____ .

4. Flower pollen makes me sneeze. I have an _____ .

5. He took a big _____ of the orange cake .

6. The _____ sang a number of songs at the concert.

choir   allergy   candle   table   lined   freight   mouthful

 **Write**

Listen to the sentences twice, then try to write them down. The first one has been done for you.

CD 5
Track 50

For teacher's marks only.

1. She scraped her knee.

2. _____

3. _____

4. _____

5. _____

6. _____

7. _____

8. _____

 Listen & write

Listen again if you need to. You can spell a lot of words now and write whole sentences. Well done!

 Test me!

79

Certificate!

This is to certify that

....

has finished

LETTERLAND® Fix-it Phonics Level 3

....

Your Letterland Teacher

....

Date

www.letterland.com